A Commitment to Unleash Your Leader Potential

Follow a Five-Step Process That Will Help You
Find Success, Significance, and Satisfaction

DANIEL W. EVANS

WESTBOW·
PRESS
A DIVISION OF THOMAS NELSON
& ZONDERVAN

WestBow Press books may be ordered through booksellers or by contacting:

WestBow Press
A Division of Thomas Nelson & Zondervan
1663 Liberty Drive
Bloomington, IN 47403
www.westbowpress.com
1 (866) 928-1240

Because of the dynamic nature of the Internet, any web addresses or links contained in this book may have changed since publication and may no longer be valid. The views expressed in this work are solely those of the author and do not necessarily reflect the views of the publisher, and the publisher hereby disclaims any responsibility for them.

ISBN: 978-1-4908-2527-4 (sc)
ISBN: 978-1-4908-2526-7 (hc)
ISBN: 978-1-4908-2528-1 (e)

Library of Congress Control Number: 2014902032

Printed in the United States of America.

WestBow Press rev. date: 4/15/2014

Interior design by Daniel W. Evans.

Daniel Evan's latest work, *A Commitment to Unleash Your Leader Potential*, boldly cuts through the confusion and the excuses of playing safe and small as a leader. His words provide a clear path for a new type of leadership—*unleashed!* Read it and you will be motivated and educated to embrace your potential.

Dr. Kary Oberbrunner, author, coach, speaker
Igniting Souls, Columbus, Ohio

It is… great for aspiring leaders and people who want to be better leaders. The author has done a good job … and I believe it will be of immense benefit to readers. It is a good contribution to the growing body of leadership resources.

Dr. Francis Bola Akin-John
International Church Growth Ministry, Lagos, Nigeria

I am excited to have a ready-to-use resource to share with the leaders in my organization. *A Commitment to Unleash Your Leader Potential* is an excellent personal development tool for leaders, centered on an ancient spiritual discipline. *A Commitment to Unleash Your Leader Potential* is an easily implemented tool that moves leaders toward reproducing themselves in others, which is the ultimate measure of a leader.

—Dave Bowman, senior pastor
New Horizons Church, Durham, North Carolina

I myself am confident that God is talking to certain people, like my friend Daniel Evans, to write books like this one to help prepare leaders to be strong and help them to keep the Faith, because of the things we are about to go through in the last days. I thank God my brother is Holy Spirit led.

Roy Allen, pastor
Imprint Ministries, Winter Haven, Florida

The Intent of This Book

As a leader, I have learned many lessons. Some of them even took me through the school of hard knocks. Even though being dragged to the woodshed would have been a bed of roses compared to some of my life's lessons, they have prepared me for future lessons. Can you relate?

We all know life has its twists and turns. Even for a leader, life does not have mercy. For this reason, I have written this book.

We all make commitments and then are tempted to break them. Sometimes the decisions to keep them are more than we care to accept. It would be easier to say, "Okay, let me out of here and give me some air." Remember, quitters never win. They lose by default. They do not lead well either. If they lead, their following is small.

Following the methodologies in this book will help you unleash your leadership potential. This book will challenge you. At the same time, it will offer insight and bring clarity. What more could you ask for in personal growth?

Anyone equipped and prepared for what lies ahead is far better off. You will learn about qualities that will equip and prepare you to be confident and available.

What lies dormant within you, longing to hear the word *unleash*?

A leader can learn to increase influence. This book will help you do just that. You will learn to monitor and produce measurable results.

The book's title is *A Commitment to Unleash Your Leader Potential.* Are you ready to learn how to unleash yours? It will involve a commitment. The level of commitment you make and maintain will determine your success.

Contents

Chapter 1

Experience and Influence

Are you ready to learn how to be more successful and significant? Do you maintain satisfaction in the midst of growing pains? You will be able to answer these questions and more in one day.

This one-day process takes you through five steps. The practicality of the steps helps bring clarity and revelation. Dedicate one day to this, and you will glean from it for many days.

The Five Steps

Step One—Stay Focused
Step Two—Make Commitments
Step Three—Implement Structure
Step Four—Learn to Glean
Step Five—Measure Up

Personal Experience

Since 1982, I have regularly enjoyed the practice of fasting. These endeavors consisted of not eating for a meal at a time to days, and even weeks. Whether I chose to not eat for a meal or other lengths of time, I spent the time praying instead. This discipline proves to be very rewarding.

A partial to complete abstinence from food has always been a part of my fasting periods. I also include the sacrifice of other activities and pleasures. Chapter five lists a few scriptural examples with explanations such as music, sleep, and so on. The act of self-denial is very beneficial for my mind, body, and relationship with God.

While I fast, my focus is on strengthening and deepening my relationship with God. The world or my body's fleshly desires are of much less concern.

Over the years, my studies of fasting in the Word of God taught me much. The practical experience is more important than naming specific biblical fasting examples. Many do this expecting the same results.

For example, arbitrarily naming a fast, such as a "Daniel Fast" will not present an understanding of visions (Daniel 10). However, it will assist you in developing the kind of character Daniel possessed. Practicing this discipline prepares you to receive from God, as he and many other biblical characters did through fasting.

As you read further, I will cite biblical examples of people who fasted and received from God. These examples are not meant to set a standard. They serve to enlighten you by highlighting the important benefits of denying the flesh and seeking God.

I teach on this subject and reference it in preaching on many occasions. The concept of fasting guides came when I prepared a structured fasting program for my home church. When I started writing, there was a constant flow from the Holy Spirit until it was completed.

During the fast, the Lord prompted me to publish a book. The purpose is for others who seek a structure to help them start or continue fasting. This book offers many scriptural helps and explanations.

During my own fasts, the importance of both structure and keeping a journal became evident. I provide this structured system to aid you in your fasting experience. The structure is meant to enhance your fasting experience. The intent is not only to increase your understanding, but also to develop servitude through this discipline.

This discipline helps develop an intimate and personal relationship with the Father, Son, and Holy Spirit. You learn to submit yourself to God by saying no to the flesh.

Leadership Influence

This book is specifically for the leader in each of us. You may ask, "Who me?" Yes, this includes you! When you think about it, every person living is a leader. It may be in a positive or a negative way, but you lead others by influencing them.

Your influence consists of four areas. They are somebody, sometime, somewhere, in some way, which I call the Four Areas of Leadership Influence.

Let's review the four areas.

Somebody – You influence somebody. Identify the people you influence within your inner circles. Are there other regular associations who are not in your inner circles? Examples could be coworkers, neighbors, and so on. Then you need to determine whether you influence these people negatively or positively. As you define and refine your leadership skills within the other areas, your *"Somebody"* following will expand.

Remember, when you add value to others, you are also adding value to yourself. Your legacy is not determined by the size of your following, but the impact you made in each individual. Your epitaph will not be what is written on a marble monument. But what is remembered, shared and applied every day in the lives of the living.

Sometime – You influence somebody sometime. What are the times of the day, days of the week, weeks of the month, or months of the year you positively influence your "Somebody" people the most. The proper *"Sometime"* for the greatest positive influence is when we are at our peak performance. Are you approachable before your first cup of coffee? What do neighbors and family think of you after a stressful day? These questions are in reference to your attitude at certain times.

There are times in our lives when we may influence negatively. For some it could be seasonal and for others more frequent. Your negative seasons could be short or long periods.

We must recognize and acknowledge our positive *"Sometime"* seasons and maximize the opportunities. This process of recognizing and acknowledging will give you clarity of any negativity as well.

Somewhere – You influence somebody, sometime, somewhere. Where do you influence people the most? Is it at home, work, church, community events, a friend's house, or maybe as a radio or TV spokesperson? These are different examples of places and the environments are even more diverse.

Everyone should have a sense of comfort at home for personal expression. A family member or friend's home may not offer the same level of comfort, but could be similar. On the other hand, the workplace, churches, and community events could be very different. The differences may vary in the amount of people present, hours of operation, and the potential of responsibilities. Even the example of a radio or TV spokesperson is different because your "Somebody" following could be people you never meet.

Your level of self-confidence and experience will determine how effective you are in your "*Somewhere*" area of influence. Whether a small or large group or people you may never meet, developing your leadership skills will empower you to add value.

Some way – You influence somebody, sometime, somewhere, in some way. In what ways do you influence? Is it your charismatic personality? Could it be your management of business and finances? Maybe the way you make time for people or the constant smile you wear. We could go on with examples of how you may influence even to the negative side. We have shared enough to prove the point that we influence people in many ways.

A positive influence is always good and adds value. In others, your "*Some ways*" can promote self-awareness and the desire to practice the same. When you take time to reflect and determine your positive ways you establish self-value. Keep in mind that these ways are channels used to add value to others. Do not allow a channel blockage. It will affect your self-value and the potential of adding value to others. When we are aware and have knowledge of the ways we influence people, then we are more equipped to manage for maximum impact.

You may say, "All right, you have my attention. Where do we go from here?"

First, you must identify your four areas and your strengths. This process will also cause weakness to surface. This will allow you to maximize your "some ways" for a positive impact.

Of course, this is difficult for some to do. That is why those who have already followed the process can assist others to develop in their "some ways."

To influence others, we may need to change our ways. It is easier to change yourself than to change someone else, not to mention your "sometime" opportunities or your surroundings. We can change our ways in order to be leaders who are more effective, even at certain times and in certain surroundings.

Leaders influence others. They lead them in a specific direction in their actions, words, and thoughts. This is the reason followers must choose their leaders well.

On the other hand, leaders must know their followers. This might also include other leaders on the team. There are three choices for those who are negative influences. The first and second are to replace them or to limit how they lead. The third is the best option: assist them to identify their four areas and train them.

I believe everyone is a leader. However, not everyone recognizes or develops the four areas of leadership influence.

Do not be confused! Leadership is influence, and there are not four different influences. However, the areas of somebody, sometime, somewhere, and some way make up our overall influence. Think of how a pie can be sliced into four pieces, yet it remains one pie.

The four areas are whom we influence, when we influence, where we influence, and how we influence. Who, when, where, and how can be seen clearly. Identifying these areas will enable you to define and refine skills for greater effectiveness in each area.

Any good leader should strive to maximize his or her reach of positive influence to as many as possible. The result is an increase in the number of people in your tribe.

Some are unacknowledged leaders in their homes or among peers. They have no ambition to lead others beyond that point. They are content as a follower, without realizing they have the potential for far greater accomplishments.

Children lead other children. Parents lead the home. You may be a leader to your neighbors. A homeless person may be a leader among the homeless. If you are a reserved person with your words, you may influence impulsive talkers to be more reserved.

As Christians, we should be such godly examples that others desire a relationship with Christ. That, my friend, is influence.

There are leaders all around us and you may be one of them.

My prayer is that the Holy Spirit will enlighten you to the positive and negative aspects of your leadership qualities. Focus on when, where, and in what ways you influence others. Define and refine your skills and lead away!

Now, let's get started with your divine appointment. Focus is the place to start.

Focus, focus, and more focus!

Did I mention focus?

This is your day! Be ready for your commitment.

Chapter 2

Step One— Stay Focused

That's been one of my mantras—focus and simplicity. Simple can be harder than complex. You have to work hard to get your thinking clean to make it simple. But it's worth it in the end because once you get there, you can move mountains. —Steve Jobs

Stay focused is step one. Focus is the key to starting anything. It is also important in the process of reaching goals.

Learning to focus and maintaining that focus can be challenging at times. Life offers many distractions, and so many times, we allow them to do their job. Moving past them and staying focused is a learned ability. Be intentional in your focus and plans.

A coach asks questions to direct people in their own thought processes. This allows them to acknowledge an answer they may already know. This process helps them to focus.

Review carefully and prayerfully the questions and comments contained in this chapter. Pray and think about how you are leading.

9

Are you a leader of followers or a leader of leaders? Do you recognize the leadership qualities in your followers? Are you helping them to develop their abilities? If not, you are a leader of followers.

This kind of leadership does not allow potential leaders to develop. They will eventually go where they can receive instruction and training. Leaders of followers do not necessarily have to deliver the instruction and training; they may need assistance themselves.

A leader should follow these three simple steps. First, recognize the potential of their followers. Second, make sure the needs for instruction, training, and resources are available. Third, intentionally and actively get them engaged in the instruction and training.

We may not be able to help everyone, even those with potential. As followers, they may be completely satisfied and have no desire to take on more responsibility. However, those who receive become the fruit of our labor.

It is important to identify those soaring outside their comfort zones, seeking an opportunity. Especially recognize those expressing dissatisfaction with their current positions.

Leaders need to tap into their freewill and make proper choices. It is the responsibility of leaders to recognize leader potential in others and to produce more leaders.

God does not predestine leaders. However, He does acknowledge faith and the desire of those to promote the kingdom of God. This is true whether in the church or in the marketplace.

God possesses the ability to see into the future. He knows who the obedient by faith will be, as He did with Jeremiah (Jeremiah 1:5–10). Study these verses, and you will conclude that God knows who will make the right decisions. For example, God spoke to Jeremiah, allowing him to make the right decisions and encouraging him to obey (vv. 7–9).

As recorded in Scripture, God called five other men from birth: Samson (Judges 13:2–14, 24–25), Samuel (1 Samuel 1:17–20, 27–28), John the Baptist (Luke 1:11–17), Paul (Galatians 1:15–16), and Jesus Christ (Matthew 1:18–25). Does this mean that these were the only capable leaders in Scripture? That is definitely not the case!

God did not call Noah, Abraham, Moses, David, Daniel, Isaiah, and Jehoshaphat from birth. Neither did He call New Testament leaders such as Peter, James, John, and many others from birth. Yet they helped lead the church to a new level.

God knows who will allow his or her potential to promote him or her into leadership positions.

At what level of leadership were you when you started out? Who assisted you to become who you are today? What will you do to assist others to become all they desire to be? After praying and giving careful thought to these questions, you will likely notice leaders all around you.

The next chapter also contains questions and comments. However, these are with a design and purpose to help you realize two things. First, you did not climb the leadership ladder alone, and second, you did not progress without assistance.

With these thoughts in mind, reflect on the leaders divinely placed in your life. In addition, realize that you need to be available for the same purpose.

Chapter 3

Questions for Further Focus

Did God create humankind in His image and likeness?

Does this apply to all human beings?

Has God created some inferior?

Did God create people as equals?

Consider this: if all have the opportunity to be born
again, then all have leadership potential.

Did Christ die for some or for the entire world of whosoevers?

Does every Christian have the same opportunity in Christ?

According to His Word, is God a respecter of persons?

Are faith and the Word of God available to all?

Did Christ die for all humanity?

Who are we in Christ?

Who are *you* in Him?

You are God's special possession—

a chosen generation,

a royal priesthood,

a special people.

Christ died for all and knew that humanity has
the potential to lead and live for Him.

It has never been and will never be that our
God does not know what He is doing!

The difference is our own choices. It is
about what we do or do not do.

It is about whether we seize the opportunities available to us.

Remember that right motives produce good decisions,
which consistently produce great leaders.

It is important to answer these questions and take the comments to heart. You should be the focus. Your decisions and actions are what will affect your influence on others. You are the reason for this book.

Just to emphasize: you are a created being with the potential to live and lead with purpose. You have the potential to be much more than what many others settle for. Make the choice to be all you should be.

Daniel W. Evans

Right now, you should be able to sense the leader rising in you. You may be one who has been soaring with the eagles in your personal growth. If this is true, you will find yourself bursting at the leader seams. Making a commitment and following the structure outlined in this book is for you too. It will propel you to the slopes of Mount Leaderest!

Loosen up and get ready for your release! It is up to you. How far do you desire to go? It is time for you to make *a commitment to unleash your leader potential.*

With your thoughts in focus, let's move on.

Chapter 4

Step Two—Make Commitments

It was character that got us out of bed, commitment that moved us into action, and discipline that enabled us to follow through. —Zig Ziglar

Make commitments is step two. It starts with making a commitment for one day. This could be one of your best decisions.

Life is full of opportunities for making commitments. Some of them could bring significant changes into your life.

This book with many specific instructions will help guide you to maintain focus. Consider it as a tool to assist you in seeking God through the biblical discipline of fasting.

This discipline can assist you in identifying your God-given leadership potential. It can also assist you in developing your potential both through inherent skills and through skills you can learn.

This book also contains areas like a personal journal to help you through your one day of prayer and fasting. Record what the Holy Spirit reveals to you during these times. The revelations could be for you or for others.

Many times people neglect to write down the revelations or directions they receive from the Lord. At certain places in this book, particularly in the back, you will find instructions on what to write as well as lines to write on.

The Bible reminds us that the Lord commanded the prophets to write what they saw or heard. This was not only for their personal reference, but for future readers as well. It is crucial to keep a record of what you receive from the Lord.

If you are like some of us, you cannot always rely on your memory. When you receive life-changing revelation, the devil works overtime to bombard our minds with worldly cares. In all the confusion, Satan's efforts are certainly to help us forget.

The one-day fasting and the day after portions of this book include passages from the following Bible versions: the New International Version (NIV), the King James Version (KJV), the New American Standard Bible (NASB), the Amplified Bible (AB), and the New King James Version (NJKV). The Scriptures are marked with the abbreviation in parentheses.

The Holy Spirit may lead you to read passages before and after the listed Scripture. In doing this, you may receive instruction, rebuke, correction, revelation, or direction.

Second Timothy 3:16–17 says, "Every Scripture is God-breathed (given by His inspiration) and profitable for instruction, for reproof and conviction of sin, for correction of error and discipline in obedience,

[and] for training in righteousness (in holy living, in conformity to God's will in thought, purpose, and action), So that the man of God may be complete and proficient, well fitted and thoroughly equipped for every good work" (AB).

Second Peter 1:20–21 says, "[Yet] first [you must] understand this, that no prophecy of Scripture is [a matter] of any personal or private or special interpretation (loosening, solving). For no prophecy ever originated because some man willed it [to do so—it never came by human impulse], but men spoke from God who were borne along (moved and impelled) by the Holy Spirit" (AB).

Pray and allow the Holy Spirit to assist you regarding how you should fast and what you should sacrifice. Be sure to log each item in the proper spaces within this book.

There are spaces to record commitments for each activity, including entertainment, pleasure, and food(s) sacrificed during your fast. You can also record the times of your activities or meals, as applicable.

The food items or meals and pleasures you sacrifice are between the Holy Spirit and you.

According to Scripture, food is always involved in fasting. Therefore, whether you sacrifice activities or not, include food in your fast. Keep in mind medications, health issues, and so on. You should not do anything against your doctor's orders or your pharmacist's recommendations for medications.

Whatever your decisions may be, your commitment is what will make your fast successful.

Chapter 5

Explaining a Biblical Discipline

Read these Scriptures and comments about fasting.

But as for me, when they were sick, my clothing was sackcloth: I humbled my soul with fasting; and my prayer returned into mine own bosom. (Psalm 35:13 KJV)

> Fasting can enhance your prayers for the sick. It will also humble your soul, which is your mind, will, and emotions. Even if your prayers do not benefit others due to their sin and disobedience, God will still reward you. This is because of your mercy toward them and your commitment to the fast.

When I wept, and chastened my soul with fasting, that was to my reproach. (Psalm 69:10 KJV)

> Some use fasting to discipline themselves (the soul) and for correction in areas of sin. The Bible contains examples of repentance sought while praying and fasting. In this passage, David was facing

overwhelming troubles and not only prayed, but also fasted. Read Mark 9:29 for clarity on why fasting helps when praying.

Therefore go thou, and read in the roll, which thou hast written from my mouth, the words of the LORD in the ears of the people in the LORD's house upon the fasting day: and also thou shalt read them in the ears of all Judah that come out of their cities. (Jeremiah 36:6 KJV)

Reading Scripture is common during fasting. When combined with prayer, it can bring understanding and revelation.

It is good to read Scripture aloud during your fasting, and other times as well. It may help bring even better understanding when you hear it read or read it aloud.

Then the king went to his palace, and passed the night fasting: neither were instruments of music brought before him: and his sleep went from him. (Daniel 6:18 KJV)

When you fast, you may choose not to sleep. As the king did, you may spend time in prayer instead. Jesus did this on several occasions.

In this Scripture, music is a pleasure the king sacrificed during his fasting. Read 1 Corinthians 7:5 for another scriptural example of sacrificing pleasures while fasting.

And I set my face unto the Lord God, to seek by prayer and supplications, with fasting, and sackcloth, and ashes. (Daniel 9:3 KJV)

During prayer and fasting, seeking God should always be a top priority. It needs to be the focus during your times in your daily prayer closet as well.

Seeking God's face rather than his provision produces a deep, intimate relationship with Him. This was a normal process for Daniel while he sought God for answers.

In this chapter, Daniel is also praying and repenting for the sin of his people and himself.

In those days I Daniel was mourning three full weeks. I ate no pleasant bread, neither came flesh nor wine in my mouth, neither did I anoint myself at all, till three whole weeks were fulfilled. (Daniel 10:2–3 KJV)

Sacrificing food during prayer and fasting is a practice often mentioned in Scripture. Daniel fasted three whole weeks as he waited for an answer from the Lord.

Study Daniel 10, and you will find that God released the answer on the first day of Daniel's fast. However, battles between the angelic messenger and demons hindered the delivery of Daniel's answer for three whole weeks. Daniel remained committed to his fast and constantly sought God until he received his answer.

Moreover when ye fast, be not, as the hypocrites, of a sad countenance: for they disfigure their faces, that they may appear unto men to fast. Verily I say unto you, They have their reward. But thou, when thou fastest, anoint thine head, and wash thy face; That thou appear not unto men to fast, but unto thy Father which is in secret: and thy Father, which seeth in secret, shall reward thee openly. (Matthew 6:16–18 KJV)

> When you fast with the proper motives, you can expect answered prayers and rewards. Fasting should bring joy during and after the endeavor—a result only your faith in God can produce.
>
> Remember that you should desire rewards from God, not man. If you seek recognition from man because of pride that may be all the reward you receive.
>
> In this scripture, we find hygiene measures to obey while fasting. Fasting does affect the body. Face washing, brushing your teeth, using deodorant, brushing your hair, and using fragrances will help. You will also feel better about yourself physically. You also do not want to appear to others that you are suffering or torturing yourself.

And he said unto them, This kind can come forth by nothing, but by prayer and fasting. (Mark 9:29 KJV)

> Jesus said that you could not receive or accomplish some things without prayer and fasting. If you study Mark 9, you will see that Jesus is referring to casting out demons. Moreover, the unbelief of the disciples provoked Jesus' answer.
>
> The devil used food to cause the fall of man. It was appealing to the eye and was good to eat. Of course, the fall of man was because of Adam's sin. The devil used food to deceive Eve first, and then Adam willfully ate

of it. Therefore, it makes sense that abstinence from food can help develop our prayer life.

Faith comes by hearing the Word of God, and in like manner fasting can enhance your prayer life. Thus, we learn that the disciples' lack of faith and enhanced prayer prompted Jesus' comment.

And she was a widow of about fourscore and four years, which departed not from the temple, but served God with fastings and prayers night and day. (Luke 2:37 KJV)

Some serve God through fasting and prayers. They fast and pray for many different people. The Holy Spirit constantly presents opportunity for them to fast and pray in agreement with others.

Servants who choose to serve in this manner develop a deep and intimate relationship with God. You should desire that a disciplined practitioner of fasting intercede for you.

And Cornelius said, Four days ago I was fasting until this hour; and at the ninth hour I prayed in my house, and, behold, a man stood before me in bright clothing. (Acts 10:30 KJV)

Prayer and fasting brings not only revelations, but also specific directions and an understanding of God's will. Yet many seek His will and their own purpose with wrong motives. This causes them to become disappointed, discouraged, and confused.

Pray and fast to develop a deeper and more personal relationship with Him. This will help you find His will and purpose for your life. And you will find yourself *enjoying life with purpose.*

As they ministered to the Lord, and fasted, the Holy Ghost said, Separate me Barnabas and Saul for the work whereunto I have called them. (Acts 13:2 KJV)

> You will be more attentive to the voice of the Lord when serving Him in a fast. You will receive clarity regarding His calling and direction. And you will receive divine connections to fulfill your calling.
>
> The Lord is a respecter of faith, but not of people. When you fast, you reveal your sincerity to God, but more so to yourself. Because of this, it is easier to focus your faith and attention on the things you seek. God rewards those who diligently seek Him (Hebrews 11:6).

Defraud ye not one the other, except it be with consent for a time, that ye may give yourselves to fasting and prayer; and come together again, that Satan tempt you not for your incontinency. (1 Corinthians 7:5 KJV)

Let's look at the Amplified Bible translation of this verse.

Do not refuse and deprive and defraud each other [of your due marital rights], except perhaps by mutual consent for a time, so that you may devote yourselves unhindered to prayer. But afterwards resume marital relations, lest Satan tempt you [to sin] through your lack of restraint of sexual desire.

> Some fast from sexual relations of their marriage, but only with consent of their spouse. There must be

mutual consent. This will prevent an open door for the devil to tempt you. Do not allow your fasting to be a reason for fighting a new battle. The devil is roaming and seeking whom he may devour. Your sacrifice of food and pleasures should bring you victory, not make you a victim.

Chapter 6

Step Three— Implement Structure

The leader is the organization's top strategist ... systematically envisioning the future and specifically mapping out how to get there. —Bill Hybels

Implement structure is step three. Structure is another key to planning and achieving goals. Surely, anyone would like to be more successful. A systematic framework adds structure to produce satisfactory results. The value of this increases as you not only remain committed to your fast, but also to the structure.

Near the end of this book, you will find a place to write prayer requests. Before starting your prayer and fasting endeavor, record requests from others that you have been praying for.

As you enter this endeavor, the Holy Spirit will prompt others to give you their prayer requests. During this time, your prayers will become more intense, and you will become a stronger warrior.

As you log each request before and during your fast, intercede for these requests regularly. There are also spaces to write praise reports for answered prayers. If you are participating with a group, it is important to pray for one another fervently. Praying for one another strengthens the entire group. It also encourages one another to keep their commitments.

The enemy of your soul will attack when you sacrifice things the flesh desires. That's because he knows these sacrifices are evidence of a sincere heart.

Near the end of this book, a separate page has been set aside for you to list the name of each person in your group. There are also spaces for other necessary information about that particular individual.

You will find three boxes at the top of the "Your Fasting Day" page. The intent is for you to check whether you prayed, fasted, read and prayed Scripture, or all three.

In addition, boxes beside each Scripture are for you to check after reading and praying each one.

The intent of the guide and journal portions of this book is not to create a perfect fasting process. Neither is it a guarantee of a successful fast. Nor is it to make a spiritual giant out of you. The intent is to assist you in fulfilling your commitments by adding structure. You should retain this book of your personal information for future references, especially when you pray and fast.

This is my prayer for you as you go through your one-day fasting endeavor. "Beloved, I pray that you may prosper in every way and [that your body] may keep well, even as [I know] your soul keeps well and prospers" (3 John 1:2 AB).

I also pray you gain strength to control and maintain the appetites of your flesh. I pray that you prosper in your body, mind, and spirit.

The Lord's hand is on you to glorify Him in all you do. Continue to maintain the course while enjoying a life with purpose!

Chapter 7

Get Started with Your Commitment

I would like to recognize my fasting group partners, Frank Blalock, Bob Harvey, and Chris Thompson. We have seen the supernatural in operation in many shared fasting experiences.

And we have already prayed and fasted for you and your fasting endeavor!

Fasting is a personal discipline between you and God. However, it is also rewarding to experience God's love and power with others in a group fast.

I thank God for three of the greatest fasting partners on the planet. I believe there are many others with the same passion—those who desire to develop a deep and intimate relationship with the Father and Jesus. I look forward to sharing in a fasting group endeavor with you also.

I have learned much from these men and know they can add value to any group. Keep up the good work, my brothers. Let's share the knowledge we gain with as many as we can. Together we will serve Jesus in fasting and prayers as Anna the prophetess did.

Start date of your one-day of prayer and fasting:

____/ ____ / ____

_____

Your Signature

Your Personal Writings

List below the activities, entertainment, food(s), meals, and so on (with times, as applicable) that you will fast and/or sacrifice during your one-day of prayer and fasting.

Fasting / sacrificing items	Day, time, etc.
1. _____	_____
2. _____	_____
3. _____	_____
4. _____	_____
5. _____	_____
6. _____	_____
7. _____	_____

List below the things you are seeking God for during your endeavor of prayer and fasting.

1. _____
2. _____
3. _____
4. _____
5. _____
6. _____
7. _____
8. _____
9. _____
10. _____

Use the spaces below for additional information you need to record.

1. _____ _____

2. _____ _____

3. _____ _____

4. _____ _____

5. _____ _____

6. _____ _____

7. _____ _____

8. _____ _____

9. _____ _____

10. _____ _____

11. _____ _____

12. _____ _____

Scripture References for a One-Day Fast

The passages below support a one-day fast. It is good to follow scriptural examples and to claim, by faith, the promises as others have.

Remember, fasting is a personal service strictly between God and yourself. And the number of days is not as important as the discipline itself.

There are times when you may participate in a group fast. The group could be through your church, among friends or family, or with other Christian organizations. Even in a group setting, the endeavor remains very personal.

In these biblical fasting examples, one-day fasts occurred because of diverse circumstances. They occurred during offerings in God's house, times of repentance, mourning, and the reading of God's Word. Let's review four examples.

The first example is found in Judges 20:26 (KJV): "Then all the children of Israel, and all the people, went up, and came unto the house of God, and wept, and sat there before the LORD, and fasted that day until even, and offered burnt offerings and peace offerings before the LORD."

In this Scripture, Israel asked the Lord if they should fight against the tribe of Benjamin. They had already fought them twice and lost both times. During the prayer and fasting time, the Lord told them to fight, which led them to victory.

There may be times in our life when we seem to pray to no avail. Fasting helps us to tear through fear, frustration, and failures that could be keeping us from victory.

More times than we realize, we are our own worst enemy. When we learn to conquer that enemy, we are much less concerned with outward enemies.

In the second example, Samuel told the Israelites to repent of serving false gods and to return to the Lord. He told them that if they did, He would deliver them from the Philistines. The people confessed their sin on the day of fasting and made an offering to the Lord. "And they gathered together to Mizpeh, and drew water, and poured it out before the LORD, and fasted on that day, and said there, We have sinned against the LORD. And Samuel judged the children of Israel in Mizpeh" (1 Samuel 7:6 KJV).

The Philistines heard that Israel had prepared their armies to attack. Therefore, they gathered to attack Israel. When the children of Israel found out, they were afraid, and Samuel prayed.

God sent a great thunder to frighten the Philistines so that Israel could win. A stone to remind the Israelites was set there and named Ebenezer, which means, "Hitherto hath the Lord helped us."

Fasting enhances our prayers and helps us recognize and acknowledge our need to repent of sin. When we repent, the Lord delivers us from our enemies. The psalmist says in Psalms 46:1, "God is a very present help in trouble." Keep this important truth in mind.

In the third example, Israel chose to fast during their time of mourning. "And they mourned, and wept, and fasted until even, for Saul, and for Jonathan his son, and for the people of the LORD, and for the house of Israel; because they were fallen by the sword" (2 Samuel 1:12 KJV).

They had suffered the loss of King Saul, Jonathan, and others, whom the Philistines killed. The entire chapter is about David and Israel's grief over the death of Saul and Jonathan.

During times of grieving and emotional troubles, it is hard to eat. However, this was not the case in this passage. Israel made a conscious decision to fast until the end of the day. The intent was to show respect and honor for the slain.

As revealed in Scripture, a fast is a discipline practiced with a sincere commitment to seek God. Whether in trouble or not, we can fast and seek His peace, strength, deliverance, or word.

The Philistines gave a tremendous blow to Israel by killing the king and his sons. The Philistines continued to be a thorn in Israel's side.

In the fourth example Jeremiah 36:6 says, "Therefore go thou, and read in the roll, which thou hast written from my mouth, the words of the LORD in the ears of the people in the LORD's house upon the fasting day: and also thou shalt read them in the ears of all Judah that come out of their cities" (KJV).

All Judah was to hear what God has said. Israel was in sin. God wanted them to hear of the coming judgment if they did not turn from their evil ways.

Listen for God's voice as you read or listen to Scripture. As you do, you will become aware of areas of sin in your life. It is very important to take heed, because it is what God is saying to you. God does not desire for us to continue in sins that prevent us from receiving His promises.

His greatness resides in us, and He desires for us to release that potential for two reasons: first, to be all that we can be in Him for our own benefit, and second, to be the best example we can be for others.

God receives glory and honor when others see two things: first, how good God is in our lives and how we live for Him, and second, the blessings He bestows on us.

Let's return to the Scripture reference about reading the Word of God during a fast. Not only is prayer a vital part, but the Word of God is too. When we read the Scriptures, we can receive revelation, reproof, correction, and instruction (2 Timothy 3:16–17).

It is very important to write these things down when received. Also repent of sin so that you can pray and seek God with a clean conscience. Pray for strength and guidance. Pray for patient endurance as you walk in obedience. Pray for wisdom in applying His instructions to your life.

Fasting helps us to focus clearly and deeply on the things of God. This is far more important than just pleasing the flesh.

Your Fasting Day

Day of Fast _____ _____

                               Month   *Day*

Prayed ❑   Fasted ❑   Read and Prayed Scripture ❑

Read 2 Chronicles 20:1–29 (NIV).

> After this, the Moabites and Ammonites with some of the Meunites came to wage war against Jehoshaphat.
>
> Some people came and told Jehoshaphat, "A vast army is coming against you from Edom, from the other side of the Dead Sea. It is already in Hazezon Tamar" (that is, En Gedi).
>
> Alarmed, Jehoshaphat resolved to enquire of the Lord, and he proclaimed a fast for all Judah.
>
> The people of Judah came together to seek help from the Lord; indeed, they came from every town in Judah to seek him.
>
> Then Jehoshaphat stood up in the assembly of Judah and Jerusalem at the temple of the Lord in the front of the new courtyard and said: "Lord, the God of our ancestors, are you not the God who is in heaven? You rule over all the kingdoms of the nations. Power and might are in your hand, and no one can withstand you.
>
> Our God, did you not drive out the inhabitants of this land before your people Israel and give it forever to the descendants of Abraham your friend?

They have lived in it and have built in it a sanctuary for your Name, saying, 'If calamity comes upon us, whether the sword of judgment, or plague or famine, we will stand in your presence before this temple that bears your Name and will cry out to you in our distress, and you will hear us and save us.'

But now here are men from Ammon, Moab and Mount Seir, whose territory you would not allow Israel to invade when they came from Egypt; so they turned away from them and did not destroy them.

See how they are repaying us by coming to drive us out of the possession you gave us as an inheritance.

Our God, will you not judge them? For we have no power to face this vast army that is attacking us. We do not know what to do, but our eyes are on you."

All the men of Judah, with their wives and children and little ones, stood there before the Lord.

Then the Spirit of the Lord came on Jahaziel son of Zechariah, the son of Benaiah, the son of Jeiel, the son of Mattaniah, a Levite and descendant of Asaph, as he stood in the assembly.

He said: "Listen, King Jehoshaphat and all who live in Judah and Jerusalem! This is what the Lord says to you: 'Do not be afraid or discouraged because of this vast army. For the battle is not yours, but God's.

Tomorrow march down against them. They will be climbing up by the Pass of Ziz, and you will find them at the end of the gorge in the Desert of Jeruel.

Daniel W. Evans

You will not have to fight this battle. Take up your positions; stand firm and see the deliverance the Lord will give you, Judah and Jerusalem. Do not be afraid; do not be discouraged. Go out to face them tomorrow, and the Lord will be with you.'"

Jehoshaphat bowed down with his face to the ground, and all the people of Judah and Jerusalem fell down in worship before the Lord.

Then some Levites from the Kohathites and Korahites stood up and praised the Lord, the God of Israel, with a very loud voice.

Early in the morning they left for the Desert of Tekoa. As they set out, Jehoshaphat stood and said, "Listen to me, Judah and people of Jerusalem! Have faith in the Lord your God and you will be upheld; have faith in his prophets and you will be successful."

After consulting the people, Jehoshaphat appointed men to sing to the Lord and to praise him for the splendor of his holiness as they went out at the head of the army, saying: "Give thanks to the Lord, for his love endures forever."

As they began to sing and praise, the Lord set ambushes against the men of Ammon and Moab and Mount Seir who were invading Judah, and they were defeated.

The Ammonites and Moabites rose up against the men from Mount Seir to destroy and annihilate them. After they finished slaughtering the men from Seir, they helped to destroy one another.

When the men of Judah came to the place that overlooks the desert and looked toward the vast army, they saw only dead bodies lying on the ground; no one had escaped.

So Jehoshaphat and his men went to carry off their plunder, and they found among them a great amount of equipment and clothing and also articles of value— more than they could take away. There was so much plunder that it took three days to collect it.

On the fourth day they assembled in the Valley of Berakah, where they praised the Lord. This is why it is called the Valley of Berakah to this day.

Then, led by Jehoshaphat, all the men of Judah and Jerusalem returned joyfully to Jerusalem, for the Lord had given them cause to rejoice over their enemies.

They entered Jerusalem and went to the temple of the Lord with harps and lyres and trumpets.

The fear of God came on all the surrounding kingdoms when they heard how the Lord had fought against the enemies of Israel.

To many, this is a favorite fasting Scripture because it indicates that the supernatural is at work after a fast.

After reading this chapter many times over the years, I thought I understood it well. But recently I received a revelation from the prayer of Jehoshaphat. A fast helped create the atmosphere for such a prayer. Because of fasting and prayer, we see the results of supernatural deliverance and the accumulation of wealth.

After Jehoshaphat and the people prayed and fasted, God moved in a miraculous way. They did not even have to raise a sword during this battle. When we pray and fast (take those extreme measures), God fights the battles for us.

This is great news, because God changes not! What He has done for one, He will do for another. What He has done at one time, He can certainly do again.

Let's take Him at His word and experience God moving in supernatural ways on our behalf.

A fast combined with prayer helps us in many ways supernaturally. For example, it can help meet our needs for healing, finances, deliverance, and favor. And it can help us to become better leaders.

We cannot hide anything from God. He knows our motives, inabilities, inexperience, weakness, and sin. Many are looking for wealth, others for beauty, still others for perfect health, and so on. God desires to give us our heart's desire as His Word says.

However, He would rather raise up spiritual leaders, such as Jehoshaphat—leaders who He knows will honor Him with their lives and substance, even after God gives them great wealth. The evidence was when it took three days to collect the plunder among the fallen enemy.

Let's continue to study what God has to teach us about leadership from the biblical account of Jehoshaphat. He led his people into a fast and a victorious prayer. This resulted in a supernatural deliverance and an accumulation of wealth.

Chapter 8

Step Four—
Learn to Glean

The trees that are slow to grow bear the best fruit. —Moliere (Jean-Baptiste Poquelin)

Learn to glean is step four. The success rate of acquiring knowledge little by little is far greater than trying to learn too much too quickly. Gleaning comes with a strategic plan. Acquiring small amounts allows you the time to implement your plan slowly and carefully. The definition of *glean* is to learn, discover, or find out—usually little by little or slowly.

God requires us to grow into promotions and successes. Experience, knowledge, and revelation do not come easily to novices. The Bible warns us of placing them in leadership roles.

Personal growth is very important and does not come overnight. Many try to grow too quickly and miss so much due to impatience. You can count telephone poles from a car, but from a speeding train, they look more like a picket fence.

Let's see what years of gleaning have to say about a certain biblical leader. We will then take what we learn and apply it to ourselves. We will accomplish this in a unique way to stimulate personal growth.

Jehoshaphat was told of a vast army coming to war against him. As his nature was, he enquired of the Lord and proclaimed a fast for all Judah. He did not call for a few to fast. He proclaimed a fast for all!

Let me explain what I received from Jehoshaphat's prayer before I discuss this fasting example any further.

After people came from every town to Jerusalem, Jehoshaphat prayed the following to the Lord:

> "Lord, the (1) *God of our ancestors*, are you not the (2) *God who is in heaven?* (3) *You rule over all the kingdoms* of the nations. (4) *Power and might are in your hand,* and no one can withstand you. Our God, (5) *did you not drive out the inhabitants of this land* before your people Israel and give it forever to the descendants of Abraham your friend? They have lived in it and have (6) *built in it a sanctuary for your Name,* saying, If calamity comes upon us, whether the sword of judgment, or plague or famine, we will stand in your presence before this temple that bears your Name and will cry out to you in our distress, and (7) *you will hear us and save us.* But now here are men from Ammon, Moab and Mount Seir, whose (8) *territory you would not allow Israel to invade when they came from Egypt;* so they turned away from them and did not destroy them. See how they are repaying us by coming to drive us out of the (9) *possession you gave us as an inheritance.* Our God, (10) *will you not judge them?* For (11) *we have no*

power to face this vast army that is attacking us. (12) *We do not know what to do, but our eyes are on you.*

I will share twelve excerpts from this prayer with points I have written for each excerpt. As you read the prayer, you will see the excerpts are not changed. In addition, the points are precise.

The excerpts in the prayer are in italics and numbered in parentheses. Keep in mind the numbers are not verse references, but the number of the excerpt. I also place the excerpt underneath its respective point in the following list.

Each point began to flow as the Holy Spirit gave insights into each excerpt. Struck with amazement, I noticed something phenomenal. Not only did each point speak of its respective excerpt, but also began with the letter R.

I will explain later the specific excerpts and points. In addition, I will explain why there are twelve and why they begin with the letter R.

Since David, Jehoshaphat was one of the greatest spiritual leaders of the divided kingdoms. Through his leadership skills, he led the kingdom of Judah into spiritual reforms. He was an example of acknowledging God and walking in His ways, not in the ways of Baal.

First, let's review the excerpts and the points. Study the example of each point and excerpt to understand the twelve in the list.

Example of point
Example of excerpt from Scripture

1. Remembering who God is
   God of our ancestors

2. Residing place of God
   God who is in heaven

3. Ruling all the earth's kingdoms
   You rule over all the kingdoms

4. Recognizing the power of God
   Power and might are in your hand

5. Reflecting on what God has done
   Did you not drive out the inhabitants of this land

6. Resting place for God's name
   Built in it a sanctuary for your Name

7. Responses of God expected
   You will hear us and save us

8. Restraining order from God
   Territory you would not allow Israel to invade when they came from Egypt

9. Reestablishing a claim of inheritance
   Possession you gave us as an inheritance

10. Requesting deliverance and safety
    Will you not judge them

11. Reinforcing our strength

    We have no power

12. Resolve regarding what we can do

    We do not know what to do, but our eyes are on you

The Specific Excerpts

Study the prayer and note that these twelve excerpts are the main points of the prayer. And remember that the Holy Spirit prays for us when we do not know how or what to pray (Romans 8:26). Trusting the Lord allows the Spirit to help us in our prayer life and every other area.

The level of trust expressed in this passage was the result of what took place during the reign of Jehoshaphat. He walked in the ways of the Lord and did what he could to help bring revival. During tough circumstances, opportunities for the Holy Spirit to speak through us present themselves.

Jehoshaphat was an exemplary leader. He did not ask anyone else to pray. He prayed himself. Because of this, the Holy Spirit led him in a powerful prayer.

The Number Twelve

Let's review the importance of why there were twelve excerpts followed by twelve points. Is there any significance to the number twelve?

The number twelve is central in Scripture. It speaks of governmental perfection or order. It also speaks of divine authority. We will review this in more detail later. But first we will review the spiritual significance of the number.

In respect to symbolism, in Scripture, twelve is a perfect number, mainly because of the twelve tribes of Israel. First, they represent the twelve sons of Jacob, whose name changed to Israel. Second, the twelve tribes formed the nation Israel.

Many other examples in the Bible are patterned after the twelve tribes. Moses built twelve pillars (representing the tribes) on Mount Sinai (Exodus 24:4). Twelve spies (one from each tribe) went to spy out the Promised Land (Deuteronomy 1:23).

Twelve stones were set up as a memorial after Israel crossed the Jordan River (Joshua 4:3). Twelve stones attached to the priest's breastplate represented the names of the twelve tribes (Exodus 39:8–14).

The book of Revelation states there are twelve gates to the heavenly city. There are twelve angels at the gates. Written on the gates are the names of the twelve tribes (Revelation 21:12). The gates are twelve pearls (Revelation 21:21). The walls are made of twelve foundations, which bear the names of the twelve apostles (Revelation 21:14). The Tree of Life will bear twelve kinds of fruit for each of the twelve months (Revelation 22:2).

This is only a short list of the use of the number twelve in Scripture. We can clearly see the number twelve is significant in biblical history and prophecy.

Let's review some examples of the number twelve in respect to divine government, order and authority. Jesus chose twelve disciples, who carried His teaching to many. There are twelve apostles in the New Testament. The twelve apostles will sit on twelve thrones and judge the twelve tribes of Israel (Matthew 19:28).

Solomon had twelve officers, or commissaries, ruling his household (1 Kings 4:7). There were twelve sons of Jacob in the Old Testament. These formed the twelve tribes of Israel.

New Jerusalem will have twelve foundations and twelve gates made of twelve pearls. In addition, twelve angels will guard its gates. The city will be foursquare, with 12,000 furlongs for each side, and the wall will be 144 (twelve by twelve) cubits high (Revelation 21:16–17).

There will be 144,000 servants of God. This number represents 12,000 from each of the twelve tribes of Israel. God will place a seal on their foreheads. They are to be witnesses during the Great Tribulation.

Today, our society uses this number in a variety of ways. There are twelve people on a jury. A dozen is twelve. A foot has twelve inches. There are twelve grades in school. A twelve-hour day and a twelve-hour night make up a twenty-hour period. The twelve-hour day and twelve-hour night is not only recognized today but was also recognized in biblical times.

So we can conclude in this brief study that the number twelve is biblically, historically, socially, and prophetically significant.

Can you begin to see why there are twelve points to Jehoshaphat's prayer? Can you also see that he strove to operate his government in divine perfection and order? Jehoshaphat yielded to divine authority. This provided him with authority and allowed him to delegate authority to others for leading God's people.

We could spend many hours on this subject. However, I think we have enough to see why there were twelve points in the prayer: Jehoshaphat was operating in divine authority. He was a righteous king who led his people into righteousness. He honored God. He prayed and believed for an answer. He trusted God for deliverance. He fasted by denying his propensities, so he could focus on God unhindered.

The deliverance of Israel and the accumulation of wealth were the results of obedience to God's instructions.

<u>Do your prayers line up with Jehoshaphat's prayer</u>? Do your prayers open the door for the supernatural to operate? If not, praying and fasting is one very good way to start.

The Letter R

Why do all the points start with the letter R? I might easily say there is a supernatural reason that they start with the letter R. However, I cannot.

I can explain it by using the twentieth letter of the Hebrew alphabet known as *Resh* (*raysh*). The pictograph image of this letter is a bowed head. It depicts a chief, someone at the top, and the acknowledgment of a state of servitude. The image represents the place of illumination and alludes to the source of intellect, reason, and wisdom.

This all sounds good, but I cannot use this Hebrew letter as an explanation either. Besides, the points came to me in English, not in Hebrew.

So, why do the points start with the letter R? I had typed several points and had others in mind before I noticed they started with the same letter. As with the number twelve, it is spiritually significant that these points started in this fashion.

I also believe the excerpts from the prayer are significant. Therefore, the entire body of the prayer revolves around these excerpts.

The beginning words of each point are *remembering, residing, ruling, recognizing, reflecting, resting,* and *responses.* The remaining words are *restraining, reestablishing, requesting, reinforcing,* and *resolve.* I did not notice this at first. However, after some study and meditation, I knew what the Holy Spirit desired for me to share about these points.

Look at the R words above again. They are all positive words. Not one of them is a negative word of doom and gloom. These words can add value to a person. They are words that edify, educate, enable, encourage, energize, enlarge, enlighten, equip, and exhilarate.

Our focus has been moving toward leadership. God desires to make us all better leaders. As disciples make disciples, God desires for leaders to make leaders.

Let's briefly study each word.

Remembering and *reflecting* speak of recalling from memory. This is a good process to help you learn from history and move ahead by setting new goals.

Specific exercises are required to develop and maintain a satisfactory level of memory. This is not in reference to physical exercise, because it may require slowing down and sometimes even stopping for proper reflection. Many times clarity is not available because we are not fully engaged in the process.

Residing speaks of remaining in one place due to being vested and secure. A good leader never runs from problems or people. The investment of money, time, relationship, and responsibility gives him a sense of security and steadfastness.

Ruling speaks of having control. You need control of your life and your dreams. In fact, temperance, or self-control, is one of the ninefold fruit of the Spirit (Galatians 5:23).

Can you control and manage yourself? Can you control and manage your home? If you cannot control and manage these, how can you be an effective leader of others?

Recognizing speaks of the ability to identify and follow up with an acknowledgment. It is important for leaders to recognize their leadership influence and acknowledge their weakness in the four areas discussed in chapter one.

The Four Areas of Leadership Influence is that we influence somebody, sometime, somewhere and in some way. Our "some ways" are the ways we influence others. This is the most important area of the four to identify. Once identified and acknowledged we can develop and grow in each positive way of our "some ways." This in turn will help us develop in our leadership skills. A leader's personal growth is an important factor in his effectiveness.

Resting speaks of refreshing yourself. Many times a leader's encouragement and strength to continue the course come out of rest. Be thankful for those who continually encourage you to slow down and take rest.

The physical body and the mind require rest to recuperate. We must be mentally alert and physically able to meet the demands of our leadership.

Responses speak of communication and interaction. The most effective communication is two-way, which consists of talking and listening. This is true interaction that involves respect for the other.

Communication is vital to the growth of any organization or individual. There must also be a balance between talking and listening.

Restraining speaks of control over impulsiveness. A learning model established on action without thought, especially for nonemergencies, is never good.

A leader must be aware of the example he sets for his followers. Impulsiveness is an enemy to setting and accomplishing goals that positively influence the team. Be intentional and strategic in planning and setting goals. This will lead to growth.

Reestablishing speaks of validating an already settled and accepted position. It also speaks to proving the truth of a matter or reconfirming something that should already be acknowledged.

A leader and his followers can share a sense of acceptance and approval. The leader should regularly validate his position. A settled and established leader accomplishes this task by being active in his responsibility and authority.

Complacency and lethargy are enemies to a leader. If either of these exists, actions based on responsibility may not be prevalent.

Requesting speaks of polite demands. The attitude and responses of a leader are very important in developing new leaders. Leaders must be polite and set an example for his followers. This helps maintain harmony so that goals can be accomplished. This is critical, especially if followers are volunteers, but can also help maintain productivity and manage costs when dealing with employees.

Reinforcing speaks of strengthening for more effectiveness. A great leader should constantly examine himself for effectiveness.

He must be willing to make investments in his personal growth in additional training and continuing education. If influence is low, so is effectiveness. They go hand in hand. If a leader desires to strengthen his tribe and increase his reach, he must increase his influence.

Resolve speaks of purposeful decisiveness. Life is full of decisions, and effective leaders are decisive.

If time allows, a leader should engage his team in gathering information for making decisions. This could also allow the team to share in making those decisions.

Make wise and educated decisions on purpose, and train delegated leaders to do the same. Doing nothing is still a decision. The best decisions are those that rely on intentionality and information, not on fear and lack of knowledge.

* * *

Now that we have reviewed each word, we can clearly see that the Holy Spirit inspired these R words. They add value for character building and leadership skill development.

The twelve excerpts and points reveal God's desire for us as leaders. Jehoshaphat desired to serve God and lead the people of his kingdom to do the same. He was definitely like his great-great-great-great-grandfather David, a man after God's own heart.

I have two beliefs about this brief study on leadership. First, inspiration assisted Jehoshaphat to bring revelation through prayer to the saints of old and the saints of today. Second, inspiration helped me find the excerpts and gave me the points that added additional revelation.

The Holy Spirit inspires us and gives us revelation according to the following two passages of Scripture:

> Every Scripture is God-breathed (given by His inspiration) and profitable for instruction, for reproof and conviction of sin, for correction of error and discipline in obedience, [and] for training in righteousness (in holy living, in conformity to God's will in thought, purpose, and action), So that the man of God may be complete and proficient, well fitted and thoroughly equipped for every good work. (2 Timothy 3:16–17 AB)

> [Yet] first [you must] understand this, that no prophecy of Scripture is [a matter] of any personal or private or special interpretation (loosening, solving).For no prophecy ever originated because some man willed it [to do so—it never came by human impulse], but men spoke from God who were borne along (moved and impelled) by the Holy Spirit. (2 Peter 1:20–21 AB)

Therefore, Jehoshaphat and I both received inspiration. The Holy Spirit moved on us so that one would pray and the other receive revelation.

God's desire for us is to place Him above all things, even the appetites of the flesh. Fasting is a discipline that helps us not to yield to our propensities and brings clarity when God speaks. This allows freedom from hindrances that prevent us from walking in the supernatural.

Jehoshaphat's Godly Actions

Jehoshaphat was a good king who ruled over the kingdom of Judah. His desire was to serve God and walk in the ways of the Lord. Following the ways of the Lord brought religious reform to the land.

Jehoshaphat not only refused to seek Baal, he also destroyed the high places and groves used for Baal worship. His goal was to lead the people from Baal worship back to worshiping the God of Judah.

He sent teachers who were men of God to teach in all the cities (2 Chronicles 17:7–9). These measures brought Judah back to God and helped bring about the reform. This caused the surrounding nations to fear and not war against Jehoshaphat.

The Philistines, an old enemy, sent expensive gifts to Jehoshaphat because he was increasing in greatness. Commerce was good, and mighty men of valor were in Jerusalem. The economy and military were looking good.

But he made a wrong decision: he joined with Ahab, the king of Israel, in a war against the Syrians. When Ahab asked Jehoshaphat to join him, false prophets lied to Jehoshaphat, telling him he should go with Ahab. However, Jehoshaphat wanted another opinion. Micah came and gave the word of the Lord, and Ahab disapproved and threw Micah in prison.

Jehoshaphat joined in battle with Ahab against Micah's counsel. When in battle Ahab disguised himself. The Syrians assumed Jehoshaphat was the king of Israel. When he cried to the Lord for help, the Lord delivered him. And despite his disguise, Ahab was wounded and died.

Jehoshaphat's failures did not hinder him from achieving his goals to promote the kingdom of God. He knew God was angry, but he did not allow this knowledge to deter him. He knew he had made a mistake and needed a new direction.

Some will not only throw in the towel, but also wrap a brick in it. The intent would be to get the towel further from them. I hope you are not one of them. Even if you are, there are always other options. One is to do as Jehoshaphat did and not cry over spilled milk. Shake it off and keep moving forward.

This is a great example of *failing forward*. Failure is not a permanent stopping point, but a new starting point. You just may have to change your direction.

God allows failure at times if it will get us moving forward again. All leaders face failure, but the difference is how they react to it. On the highway of success, failure is not a caution sign, but a stop sign. At the stop sign of failure, we need to stop, reflect, and then continue in a new direction.

In chapter 19 of 2 Chronicles, Jehoshaphat returned to Jerusalem in peace. The Lord was angry with him for joining himself with a king that hated Him. But because of all the good he had done, God still blessed his reign.

Jehoshaphat appointed judges throughout the land to mediate religious and kingdom issues. The chief priest handled religious matters and a ruler of Judah kingdom matters. Jehoshaphat also decreed that the judges take no bribes. They were not to judge in respect of man. They were to judge with the fear of the Lord and with a perfect heart.

Thus the people desired the things of God, and revival flourished. The kingdom of Judah prospered in the Lord due to Jehoshaphat's rule. He was one of the good and righteous kings of the divided kingdoms.

This was also during the time when the twelve tribes existed as two kingdoms. The kingdom of Israel consisted of ten tribes and the kingdom of Judah of two tribes. The kingdom of Israel had more kings that did not follow the Lord and were unrighteous. This resulted in trouble and hardships for the people.

The kingdom of Judah had many righteous kings who led the people to the Lord. Jehoshaphat was one of those kings.

What can we learn from these kingdoms and their leaders? A leader who trusts the Lord for guidance and utilizes Godly wisdom will positively influence their followers. His decisions will allow a release of blessings on the people and the land.

Jehoshaphat was an excellent example of a good leader. He first determined direction and vision, and then shared it with the people. He added value to everyone by sharing the same knowledge. He did this by providing teachers. He also held himself and everyone else accountable by appointing judges.

Jehoshaphat took time for himself and the people to reflect. Reflection allowed them to remember where they came from and where they could be. His prayer revealed this by reminding God that He gave them the land.

He recognized the kingdom's limitations by saying he had no power and did not know what to do. He set the example of what to do after he acknowledged the limitations. He then drew from his strengths.

Daniel W. Evans

This assisted him to look for sources to help develop himself beyond his limitations. He accomplished this by saying, "Our eyes are on You." He knew where his help would come from.

Meditate on these questions:

- Who has His eyes on you?
- Who are your eyes on?

Chapter 9

Leadership Qualities That Promote Growth

Quality is an essential or distinctive characteristic, property, or attribute. The qualities listed in this chapter are essential and distinctive to your leadership.

Let's take the twelve points and compare them with twelve leadership qualities. A leader who develops toward possessing and leading with these qualities will also produce strong teams.

Leaders have followers. A good leader recognizes potential leaders. He then incorporates skills into his team of leaders, training them in these same skills.

Team energy and participation increases with proper assessments and with more involvement of the leader. Jehoshaphat practiced this in a corporate fast (2 Chronicles 20). God as the ultimate mentor, trainer, and leader equipped Jehoshaphat to be a great leader of influence.

These following twelve qualities must be evident in your organization. If they are not, apply skills to produce them in the leadership of your organizations. They will help your team be more proactive and productive.

Study these twelve leadership qualities and reflect on your own to see if any need improving. If you identify weakness or if you do not possess certain qualities, there is hope. In the next chapter, you will learn to implement a plan to produce measurable results.

It is important not to think of others but only of yourself during this process.

Leadership Qualities

Prayer Point	*Leadership Quality*
1. Remembering who God is	You are an established and recognized mentor. With positive influence, you have left a permanent imprint by setting the example of "what is." It is what it is. You are who you are.

Quality Explanation: An *establisher* is someone who has become recognized and accepted. He has marked his territory. There are no misunderstandings, because points are clear, boundaries are set, and there is no information withheld.

2. Residing place of God

    You are steadfast and well positioned. You are not easily swayed and manipulated. You know your place, and you are confident in it.

    Quality Explanation: A *person of steadfastness* is firmly fixed in place or position. He knows his place, embraces it, and appreciates it. This person normally would have a strong sense of confidence in his position.

3. Ruling all the earth's kingdoms

    You are responsible for whatever it takes to meet any set goal. Your responsibility goes further than just yourself, but to the team as a whole.

    Quality Explanation: A *person of responsibility* is someone who is also accountable. This is true only for something within his power, control, or a management role.

4. Recognizing the power of God

    You acknowledge that you have the ability to use your influence. You are also able to identify areas needing action and take steps to act.

    Quality Explanation: An *influence enhancer* is someone who can increase the effect he has on another person or thing.

5. Reflecting on what God has done — You reflect to produce greater successes, and you lead your team to value the process of reflection.

> **Quality Explanation:** A *person of reflection* is someone who intentionally involves himself in long considerations or thought. This usually involves contemplating on historical facts, mostly from memory. These historical facts of reflection help in setting new goals.

6. Resting place for God's name — You are a person of reputation with integrity. You have interactions with others, and you respect them. In turn, this typically gains you the respect of others.

> **Quality Explanation:** A *person of reputation* is held in high opinion or esteem by others.

7. Responses of God expected — You are a credible, accountable, and dependable communicator.

> **Quality Explanation:** A *communicator* is a person who imparts knowledge or exchanges thoughts, feelings, or ideas. This process is through speech, writing, gestures, and so on.

Daniel W. Evans

| 8. | Restraining order from God | You rely on your wisdom and that of others. This often leads to good decisions and future successes. |

Quality Explanation: A *person of wisdom* is someone possessing the ability to think and act utilizing several mental strengths. This would involve knowledge, understanding, common sense, and insight. Wisdom offers restraint, which prevents unnecessary and hasty decisions.

| 9. | Reestablishing a claim of inheritance | You regularly rehearse the possession of a dream and actively engage in fulfilling it. |

Quality Explanation: A *dreamer* is also a visionary. Others often consider his ideas or projects audacious or too speculative. However, they are attainable.

| 10. | Requesting deliverance and safety | You overcome obstacles to promote team development while delivering control politely. |

Quality Explanation: An *overcomer* is a victorious person. This leader does not allow roadblocks to keep him from moving ahead. He normally has experience in dealing with potential failure.

| 11. | Reinforcing strengths | You are an effective encourager and supporter, and you often enhance your authority with team involvement. |

Quality Explanation: An *encourager* stimulates someone to do something by approval, assistance, or support. This leader promotes team energy, involvement, planning, and implementation.

12. Resolve regarding what we can do — You are confident. You are equipped and ready to lead with determination to strengthen your team. You are ready to identify and produce leaders from your team.

Quality Explanation: An *equipper* helps others to develop abilities, increase understanding, and whatever else is necessary and possible to achieve goals. This leader produces leaders for the purposes of organizational growth.

During your prayer and fasting period, focus on the qualities you need to develop, and ask God for help.

Use the chart in the next chapter to measure your qualities. Afterward, pray over your discoveries and take the necessary action to improve. Allow this time of fasting to help you to become more sensitive to the Spirit guiding you through this process. The results could be astounding.

Write down the people and things revealed to you. The people revealed could help springboard you into your next level of potential. In like manner, there may be things revealed that need changing. These things may be hindering you from getting closer to your dream.

Remember, you can become the family, community, workplace, and church leader that you and God desire.

*List below the revelations received; commitments or vows made;
sins revealed and repented of; life directions found; callings, gifts, or
talents discovered and so on, during this day of prayer and fasting.*

_____

_____

_____

_____

_____

_____

_____

_____

_____

For additional space, use the sheets provided in the back of this book.

Chapter 10

Step Five— Measure Up

Don't measure yourself by what you have accomplished, but by what you should have accomplished with your ability. —John Wooden

Measure up is step five. Do you measure up? What are the standards you use to measure yourself? Do you compare yourself to others? Paul says it is not wise when people compare themselves among themselves (2 Corinthians 10:12). There are higher standards for us.

In addition, we do not know what another person had to do to get where he is. There are so many variables, including experience, knowledge, beliefs, and even mentors and advisers. Negative influence could be a factor too, not to mention bad or delayed decisions.

In no way do I mean to insinuate that we should not have examples in our life. Our mentors are there for a reason. However, we cannot compare ourselves to them. We should glean from them, but not attempt to be them.

In this step, we learn the importance of measuring up. It is of the utmost importance that you compare yourself to yourself. Someone else may not be like you at all. However, he may be someone you want to be like. Learn to apply what he has done to be who he is, but be yourself. When you follow this pattern, you will have fewer disappointments, which will lead to positive results. The proper type of measuring up produces confidence and success.

We will keep it simple. What is the correct phrase for the KISS acronym? It is not "Keep it simple, stupid." For the serious leader, it cannot stand alone, and two words *must* follow. When you follow simple approaches, KISS *will come. Keep it simple; success will come!*

You will learn a simple process that will help you acknowledge the fact of your individuality. You can use this process in so many ways to help you be you.

Using the Measuring Chart exercise, examine yourself for each of the qualities and rate them individually. Evaluate and rate each one on the left by using the number scale on the right.

The number scale represents one as being "weak" and ten as being "strong." You will circle the number that represents your rating of that particular quality. Then you will be the judge of whether you need to apply action or not. However, if a rating is five or less, you may need to make an important decision. What is acceptable to you?

Personal growth should be important to a leader. If you are trying to determine whether you are a leader or not, remember that anyone can better himself. Personal growth will definitely point you toward an awareness and acknowledgement of your strengths and weaknesses.

If average is not acceptable and improvement is necessary, taking no action is not an option. Determine a proper course of action to improve each quality. Then reevaluate and rate them monthly for four months. This process of follow-up will assist you in determining two things: first, if there is any improvement, and second, if you need to change your action or continue with the same.

During your monthly follow-up evaluation, you will place a circle around the number that represents your current rating. With proper action applied, you will see a progression of success reflected by the circled numbers. Also write the date above the circled number. This will help you track your progress.

There should be a noticeable change in your follow-up test. However, some qualities may require continued action to produce measurable results. If necessary, continue your follow-up longer than the recommended four months to reach your goals.

Complete all twelve qualities in the chart. If action is necessary, fill in the blank by writing how you hope to achieve your desired results. If you are satisfied with the rating and no action is necessary, there is no need to fill in the blank.

For accountability, consider having someone who knows you well rate you. Let him rate you during each follow-up as well. This will help you reach your goals sooner. This is a good way to influence them to do the same.

You could also use this chart for leadership training by customizing it for the group's needs. See how you measure up by "measuring up."

Measuring Chart

Circle the number that represents your rating for that particular quality.

==

Establisher   1   2   3   4   5   6

                      7   8   9   10

Write action necessary for improvement

==

Person of Steadfastness   1   2   3   4   5   6

                      7   8   9   10

Write action necessary for improvement

==

Person of Responsibility   1   2   3   4   5   6

                      7   8   9   10

Write action necessary for improvement

==

Influence Enhancer	1	2	3	4	5	6
	7	8	9	10		

Write action necessary for improvement

==

Person of Reflection	1	2	3	4	5	6
	7	8	9	10		

Write action necessary for improvement

==

Person of Reputation	1	2	3	4	5	6
	7	8	9	10		

Write action necessary for improvement

==

Communicator	1	2	3	4	5	6
	7	8	9	10		

Write action necessary for improvement

==

Person of Wisdom 1   2   3   4   5   6

7   8   9   10

Write action necessary for improvement

==

Dreamer   1   2   3   4   5   6

7   8   9   10

Write action necessary for improvement

==

Overcomer   1   2   3   4   5   6

7   8   9   10

Write action necessary for improvement

==

Encourager   1   2   3   4   5   6

7   8   9   10

Write action necessary for improvement

```
=================================================
```

Equipper   **1**   **2**   **3**   **4**   **5**   **6**

                        7   **8**   **9**   **10**

Write action necessary for improvement

```
=================================================
```

What does this have to do with prayer and fasting? To the serious Christian and especially Christian leader, God is the ultimate leader.

The Holy Spirit is a teacher who desires to assist and teach us about our leadership. The discipline of fasting helps us to remove hindrances and distractions and focus on Him. While fasting we are also more sensitive to the Holy Spirit, and our prayers are more intense.

This discipline and chart are useful tools to help us with two things: first, having clarity about who we are in Christ, and second, having clarity about where we are in our leadership.

This should be an intense day for you as you study to reveal the leader in you. It may be that you are a leader already and determined to invest in your personal growth. Investing is always a plus in your leadership. Just remember that there are many who may be depending on you as a leader.

Notes for the Twelve Leadership Qualities

Below, write down anything revealed to you concerning these twelve qualities. This is an important exercise, because these qualities will be valuable when you apply the law of reflection.

1. **An Establisher**

   _____

   _____

   _____

2. **A Person of Steadfastness**

   _____

   _____

   _____

3. **A Person of Responsibility**

   _____

   _____

   _____

4. **An Influence Enhancer**

   _____

   _____

   _____

5. **A Person of Reflection**

   _____

   _____

6. **A Person of Reputation**

_____

_____

_____

7. **A Communicator**

_____

_____

_____

8. **A Person of Wisdom**

_____

_____

_____

9. **A Dreamer**

_____

_____

_____

10. **An Overcomer**

_____

_____

_____

11. An Encourager

_____

_____

_____

12. An Equipper

_____

_____

_____

Additional Leadership Notes

_____

_____

_____

_____

_____

_____

_____

_____

_____

_____

_____

_____

_____

_____

_____

_____

Chapter 11

Raise Your Awareness

One should eat to live, not live to eat.
—Moliere (Jean-Baptiste Poquelin)

Day after your fasting day _____ _____

                                            Month   *Day*

Now that your fasting period is over and it is time to eat, consider eating more wisely. The following passages contain information on how we should eat, which can assist us in maintaining healthy diets. These passages are guidelines only. They are not setting rules for what you should or should not eat.

Though it's not an all-inclusive list, here are good foods to eat: green plants, fruit, plant and fruit seeds, grains, land animal meats, honey, freshwater and seawater fish with fins and scales, and only certain bread.

Leviticus 11 lists dietary restrictions for the people of Israel. Review these Scriptures listed under the heading "Old Testament Guidelines—Also Followed by Jesus."

However, in the New Testament, the rules changed for the church, according to these Scriptures: Acts 10:9–16; Romans 10:4 and 14:1–23; Galatians 3:24–26; and Ephesians 2:15. You can review them under the heading "New Testament Eating Rules."

There are two reasons we may not have the right to eat whatever we desire: first, if eating our preferred foods causes another to stumble, and second, if eating particular foods is harmful to our bodies.

On the other hand, we should have two concerns: first, how much we eat during each meal, and second, if we are overindulging in a particular food that may be harmful to our health.

Our physical appetites reveal the level of control we have over our propensity. If our appetites are out of control, our minds and mouths may be as well. Study Deuteronomy 21:20, 2 Corinthians 10:5–6, and 2 Timothy 3:1–9. Review them under the heading "Fleshly Appetites out of Control."

The discipline of fasting assists us in maintaining control over the lust of the eye and flesh. Applying today's medical advances, technological breakthroughs, and fitness awareness can help us live a healthier lifestyle too. With better eating habits and the availability of great health care, we can have longevity with a good quality of life.

This section is a reminder to take care of the only body you will ever have. Remember, your body is the temple of the Holy Spirit.

> Don't you know that you yourselves are God's temple and that God's Spirit lives in you? (1 Corinthians 3:16 NIV)

> Do you not know that your body is a temple of the Holy Spirit, who is in you, whom you have received

from God? You are not your own. (1 Corinthians 6:19 NIV)

There are two things to keep in mind concerning our bodies as temples of the Holy Spirit. First, we need to know that we will give an account and possibly suffer from the way we neglect our bodies. Second, we must learn how to become better leaders of our own proclivity.

Saying no to weakness is much better than hearing the word *no* from a physician.

Old Testament Guidelines—Also Followed by Jesus

❑ Genesis 1:29 (NIV)
> Then God said, "I give you every seed-bearing plant on the face of the whole earth and every tree that has fruit with seed in it. They will be yours for food"

❑ Genesis 9:3–4 (NASB)
> Every moving thing that is alive shall be food for you; I give all to you, as I gave the green plant. Only you shall not eat flesh with its life, that is, its blood.

❑ Deuteronomy 8:7–9 (AB)
> For the Lord your God is bringing you into a good land, a land of brooks of water, of fountains and springs, flowing forth in valleys and hills; A land of wheat and barley, and vines and fig trees and pomegranates, a land of olive trees and honey; A land in which you shall eat food without shortage and lack nothing in it; a land whose stones are iron and out of whose hills you can dig copper.

❑ Leviticus 3:17 (NKJV)

This shall be a perpetual statute throughout your generations in all your dwellings: you shall eat neither fat nor blood.

❑ Leviticus 11:9–12 (NIV)

Of all the creatures living in the water of the seas and the streams, you may eat any that have fins and scales. But all creatures in the seas or streams that do not have fins and scales—whether among all the swarming things or among all the other living creatures in the water—you are to detest. And since you are to detest them, you must not eat their meat and you must detest their carcasses. Anything living in the water that does not have fins and scales is to be detestable to you.

❑ Deuteronomy 14:9 (NASB)

These you may eat of all that are in water: anything that has fins and scales you may eat.

❑ Luke 24:40–43 (AB)

And when He had said this, He showed them His hands and His feet. And while [since] they still could not believe it for sheer joy and marveled, He said to them, Have you anything here to eat? They gave Him a piece of broiled fish, And He took [it] and ate [it] before them.

❑ John 21:13–14 (NKJV)

Jesus then came and took the bread and gave it to them, and likewise the fish. This is now the third time Jesus showed Himself to His disciples after He was raised from the dead.

New Testament Eating Rules

☐ Acts 10:9–16 (AB)

The next day as they were still on their way and were approaching the town, Peter went up to the roof of the house to pray, about the sixth hour (noon). But he became very hungry, and wanted something to eat; and while the meal was being prepared a trance came over him, And he saw the sky opened and something like a great sheet lowered by the four corners, descending to the earth. It contained all kinds of quadrupeds and wild beasts and creeping things of the earth and birds of the air. And there came a voice to him, saying, Rise up, Peter, kill and eat. But Peter said, No, by no means, Lord; for I have never eaten anything that is common and unhallowed or [ceremonially] unclean. And the voice came to him again a second time, What God has cleansed and pronounced clean, do not you defile and profane by regarding and calling common and unhallowed or unclean. This occurred three times; then immediately the sheet was taken up to heaven.

☐ Romans 10:4 (AB)

For Christ is the end of the Law [the limit at which it ceases to be, for the Law leads up to Him Who is the fulfillment of its types, and in Him the purpose which it was designed to accomplish is fulfilled. That is, the purpose of the Law is fulfilled in Him] as the means of righteousness (right relationship to God) for everyone who trusts in and adheres to and relies on Him.

☐ Romans 14:1–23 (NASB)

Now accept the one who is weak in faith, but not for the purpose of passing judgment on his opinions. One person has faith that he may eat all things, but he who is weak eats vegetables only. The one who eats is not to regard with contempt the one who does not eat, and the one who does not eat is not to judge the one who eats, for God has accepted him. Who are you to judge the servant of another? To his own master he stands or falls; and he will stand, for the Lord is able to make him stand. One person regards one day above another, another regards every day alike. Each person must be fully convinced in his own mind. He who observes the day, observes it for the Lord, and he who eats, does so for the Lord, for he gives thanks to God; and he who eats not, for the Lord he does not eat, and gives thanks to God. For not one of us lives for himself, and not one dies for himself; for if we live, we live for the Lord, or if we die, we die for the Lord; therefore whether we live or die, we are the Lord's. For to this end Christ died and lived again, that He might be Lord both of the dead and of the living. But you, why do you judge your brother? Or you again, why do you regard your brother with contempt? For we will all stand before the judgment seat of God. For it is written, " AS I LIVE, SAYS THE LORD, EVERY KNEE SHALL BOW TO ME, AND EVERY TONGUE SHALL GIVE PRAISE TO GOD." So then each one of us will give an account of himself to God. Therefore let us not judge one another anymore, but rather determine this—not to put an obstacle or a stumbling block in a brother's way. I know and am convinced in the Lord Jesus that nothing is unclean in itself; but to him who thinks anything to be unclean, to him it is unclean. For if because of food your brother is hurt, you are no longer walking according to love. Do not destroy with your food him for whom Christ died. Therefore do not let what is for you a good thing be spoken of as evil; for the kingdom of God is not eating and drinking, but righteousness and peace and joy in the Holy Spirit. For he who in this way serves Christ is acceptable to God and approved by men. So then we pursue the things which make for peace and the building up of one another. Do not tear down the work of God for the sake of food. All things indeed are clean, but they are evil for the man who eats and gives offense. It is good not to eat meat or to drink wine, or to do anything by which your brother stumbles. The faith which you have, have as your own conviction before God. Happy is he who does not condemn himself in what he approves. But he who doubts is condemned if he eats, because his eating is not from faith; and whatever is not from faith is sin.

☐ Galatians 3:24–26 (AB)

So that the Law served [to us Jews] as our trainer [our guardian, our guide to Christ, to lead us] until Christ [came], that we might be justified (declared righteous, put in right standing with God) by and through faith. But now that the faith has come, we are no longer under a trainer (the guardian of our childhood). For in Christ Jesus you are all sons of God through faith.

☐ Ephesians 2:15 (NIV)

By setting aside in his flesh the law with its commands and regulations. His purpose was to create in himself one new humanity out of the two, thus making peace.

Fleshly Appetites out of Control

☐ Deuteronomy 21:20 (NASB)

They shall say to the elders of his city, "This son of ours is stubborn and rebellious, he will not obey us, he is a glutton and a drunkard."

❑ 2 Corinthians 10:5–6 (NIV)

We demolish arguments and every pretension that sets itself up against the knowledge of God, and we take captive every thought to make it obedient to Christ. And we will be ready to punish every act of disobedience, once your obedience is complete.

❑ 2 Timothy 3:1–9 (AB)

But understand this, that in the last days will come (set in) perilous times of great stress and trouble [hard to deal with and hard to bear]. For people will be lovers of self and [utterly] self-centered, lovers of money and aroused by an inordinate [greedy] desire for wealth, proud and arrogant and contemptuous boasters. They will be abusive (blasphemous, scoffing), disobedient to parents, ungrateful, unholy and profane. [They will be] without natural [human] affection (callous and inhuman), relentless (admitting of no truce or appeasement); [they will be] slanderers (false accusers, troublemakers), intemperate and loose in morals and conduct, uncontrolled and fierce, haters of good. [They will be] treacherous [betrayers], rash, [and] inflated with self-conceit. [They will be] lovers of sensual pleasures and vain amusements more than and rather than lovers of God. For [although] they hold a form of piety (true religion), they deny and reject and are strangers to the power of it [their conduct belies the genuineness of their profession]. Avoid [all] such people [turn away from them]. For among them are those who worm their way into homes and captivate silly and weak-natured and spiritually dwarfed women, loaded down with [the burden of their] sins [and easily] swayed and led away by various evil desires and seductive impulses. [These weak women will listen to anybody who will teach them]; they are forever inquiring and getting information, but are never able to arrive at a recognition and knowledge of the

Truth. Now just as Jannes and Jambres were hostile to and resisted Moses, so these men also are hostile to and oppose the Truth. They have depraved and distorted minds, and are reprobate and counterfeit and to be rejected as far as the faith is concerned. But they will not get very far, for their rash folly will become obvious to everybody, as was that of those [magicians mentioned].

_____

_____

_____

_____

_____

On the lines above, write revelations received; commitments or vows made; sins revealed and repented of; life directions; callings, gifts, and talents discovered; and so on.

Chapter 12

Additional Helps

The following pages are for you to record additional information from other chapters as directed.

Write your revelations, directions, commitments, and so on in the spaces below

Day and Time

1. _____   _____

   _____

2. _____   _____

   _____

3. _____   _____

   _____

4. _____   _____

   _____

5. _____   _____

   _____

Write your revelations, directions,   *Day and Time*
commitments, and so on in the
spaces below

6. _____   _____

   _____

7. _____   _____

   _____

8. _____   _____

   _____

9. _____   _____

   _____

10. _____   _____

   _____

11. _____   _____

   _____

12. _____   _____

   _____

13. _____   _____

   _____

14. _____   _____

   _____

15. _____   _____

   _____

       Daniel W. Evans

Write your revelations, directions,   *Day and Time*
commitments, and so on in the
spaces below

16. _____   _____
_____

17. _____   _____
_____

18. _____   _____
_____

19. _____   _____
_____

20. _____   _____
_____

21. _____   _____
_____

22. _____   _____
_____

23. _____   _____
_____

24. _____   _____
_____

25. _____   _____
_____

Write your revelations, directions,   *Day and Time*
commitments, and so on in the
spaces below

26. _____   _____
_____

27. _____   _____
_____

28. _____   _____
_____

29. _____   _____
_____

30. _____   _____
_____

31. _____   _____
_____

32. _____   _____
_____

33. _____   _____
_____

Write prayer requests in the spaces below.

    Name   *Prayer Request*

1. _____   _____
   _____
   _____

2. _____   _____
   _____
   _____

3. _____   _____
   _____
   _____

4. _____   _____
   _____
   _____

5. _____   _____
   _____
   _____

6. _____   _____
   _____
   _____

7. _____   _____
   _____
   _____

Name	*Prayer Request*

8. _____ _____

_____

_____

9. _____ _____

_____

_____

10. _____ _____

_____

_____

11. _____ _____

_____

_____

12. _____ _____

_____

_____

13. _____ _____

_____

_____

14. _____ _____

_____

_____

Daniel W. Evans

Name	*Prayer Request*

15. _____ _____

_____

_____

16. _____ _____

_____

_____

17. _____ _____

_____

_____

18. _____ _____

_____

_____

19. _____ _____

_____

_____

20. _____ _____

_____

_____

21. _____ _____

_____

_____

Name	*Prayer Request*

22. _____   _____

_____

_____

23. _____   _____

_____

_____

24. _____   _____

_____

_____

25. _____   _____

_____

_____

26. _____   _____

_____

_____

27. _____   _____

_____

_____

28. _____   _____

_____

_____

Name	*Prayer Request*

29. _____   _____

_____

_____

30. _____   _____

_____

_____

31. _____   _____

_____

_____

32. _____   _____

_____

_____

33. _____   _____

_____

_____

**During my day of prayer and fasting, I prayed
for each request I started with.**

Yes ❑   No ❑

**For each added request, I prayed during
my day of prayer and fasting.**

Yes ❑   No ❑

Write praise reports for answered prayers in the spaces below that correspond to the prayer requests from the previous pages.

1. _____

_____

2. _____

_____

3. _____

_____

4. _____

_____

5. _____

_____

6. _____

_____

7. _____

_____

8. _____

_____

9. _____

_____

10. _____

_____

Daniel W. Evans

Write praise reports for answered prayers in the spaces below that correspond to the prayer requests from the previous pages.

11. _____

_____

12. _____

_____

13. _____

_____

14. _____

_____

15. _____

_____

16. _____

_____

17. _____

_____

18. _____

_____

19. _____

_____

20. _____

_____

Write praise reports for answered prayers in the spaces below that correspond to the prayer requests from the previous pages.

21. _____

_____

22. _____

_____

23. _____

_____

24. _____

_____

25. _____

_____

26. _____

_____

27. _____

_____

28. _____

_____

29. _____

_____

30. _____

_____

Daniel W. Evans

Write praise reports for answered prayers in the spaces below that correspond to the prayer requests from the previous pages.

31. _____

_____

32. _____

_____

33. _____

_____

Write the names of the people from your church or group who are participating in this prayer and fasting endeavor with you.

Name   **Other Information**

1. _____   _____
   _____

2. _____   _____
   _____

3. _____   _____
   _____

4. _____   _____
   _____

5. _____   _____
   _____

6. _____   _____
   _____

7. _____   _____
   _____

8. _____   _____
   _____

9. _____   _____
   _____

Write the names of the people from your church or group who are participating in this prayer and fasting endeavor with you.

Name   **Other Information**

10. _____   _____

_____

11. _____   _____

_____

12. _____   _____

_____

13. _____   _____

_____

14. _____   _____

_____

15. _____   _____

_____

16. _____   _____

_____

17. _____   _____

_____

18. _____   _____

_____

Write the names of the people from your church or group who are participating in this prayer and fasting endeavor with you.

Name   **Other Information**

19. _____   _____

_____

20. _____   _____

_____

21. _____   _____

_____

22. _____   _____

_____

23. _____   _____

_____

24. _____   _____

_____

25. _____   _____

_____

26. _____   _____

_____

27. _____   _____

_____

Daniel W. Evans

Write the names of the people from your church or group who are participating in this prayer and fasting endeavor with you.

Name   *Other Information*

28. _____   _____
    _____

29. _____   _____
    _____

30. _____   _____
    _____

31. _____   _____
    _____

32. _____   _____
    _____

33. _____   _____
    _____

**During my day of prayer and fasting, I
prayed for each person in my group.**

Yes ❑   No ❑

Use this page for additional writing.

Daniel W. Evans

Use this page for additional writing.

About the Author

Daniel Evans is a certified coach, teacher, and speaker with the John Maxwell Team (JMT). The resources available to a JMT member are continuously expanding. These are to add value to the JMT team and the teams of the JMT members.

Daniel is also a certified speaker, trainer, and coach with the Deeper Path Team. This team offers a process to author your own "OPUS." The process consists of four elements for making your life your masterpiece.

Daniel is currently active in church leadership, business, and leadership training. He has more than thirty years of experience in each. He can lead you through the chronic pain of feeling stuck and help you reach success.

Daniel Evans
Enjoying Life with Purpose

Mailing Address: P.O. Box 61075; Durham, NC 27715 USA
Website: www.DanielEvans.org

CPSIA information can be obtained at www.ICGtesting.com
Printed in the USA
BVOW03s0600290414

351946BV00001B/2/P